Love Again After Being a Survivor of Domestic Violence

Finding Peace, Purpose, and Love After Trauma

By Milla Clervil

To every woman who thought she wouldn't make it out.
To every mother who held her children through the storm.
And to the God who held me when I couldn't hold myself.
This book is for you.

Love Again After Being a Survivor of Domestic Violence

Finding Peace, Purpose, and Love After Trauma

By Milla Clervil

Title: Love Again After Being a Survivor of Domestic Violence

Subtitle: Finding Peace, Purpose, and Love After Trauma

Chapter 1: God Gives Second Chances

I used to believe that walking away from abuse meant freedom. That once I escaped, I'd finally be able to breathe, sleep, and live again. But no one prepared me for the storm that came after the escape.

When I left my abuser, I thought I was stepping into peace. Instead, I walked into a battlefield I didn't know how to fight in. The court system cold, confusing, and cruel stripped me of the very thing I held most dear: my children. They were placed in the temporary custody of my abuser until I could prove I had a stable place to live.

The pain was indescribable. I couldn't eat. I couldn't sleep. I was losing weight so fast I barely recognized myself. The silence in my home screamed at me. My arms ached to hold my babies especially my seven-month-old, who I was still breastfeeding when they were taken from me. It felt like a part of my soul had been ripped out.

I wandered through the days like a ghost, barely functioning. Nights were the hardest. That's when the loneliness would crawl into bed with me, whispering lies that I wasn't enough. That I had failed. That maybe they were better off without me but even in that darkness, something inside me refused to die.

One morning, I stood in the mirror and saw a woman I didn't recognize tired, worn, and broken. But her eyes still had fire. I looked into that mirror and said, "If I don't fight for them, who will?" That was my turning point.

I didn't have money for a lawyer. I didn't know the legal system. I felt powerless. I try to ask people for help they sent me to place where I can get an attorney I wont have to pay but when I went to the office they told me they already helping my abuser they cannot help me. I felt like that was a knife that stabs right through my heart. I went back home I cry because I didn't really know what else to do. So I did the only thing I knew how to do I picked up the phone and called my sister. I didn't expect much. I was used to facing things alone. But when she heard my voice and I told her everything, she didn't hesitate.

She found me an attorney. Paid the full cost. And she said something I'll never forget:

"You'll pay me back when you have your life back." She believed in me when I didn't believe in myself. When the court date came, my sister drove hours to stand by my side. I walked into that courtroom terrified, but I held my head high for my children. My abuser twisted every truth. He lied with ease. Brought his cousin to speak against me. Even had a woman testify that I was mentally unstable. But I had no proof. I had only my truth.

So I spoke with dignity. I stayed calm. I told my story without anger. It was the hardest thing I've ever done speaking respectfully about a man who had brought me so much pain. But I remembered who I was fighting for: my babies and when my voice wasn't enough, God spoke for me. In that courtroom, God became my defender. While they tried to bury me in lies, God lifted the truth to the surface. Even without witnesses on my side, I began to feel peace. Because I knew the battle didn't belong to me it belonged to Him.

Eventually, I was granted 50/50 custody. It wasn't everything, but it was something. It was hope but the attacks didn't stop there. My abuser was angry. When he realized he couldn't control the courtroom, he tried to control everything else.

One morning, I opened my front door to go to church and my car was gone. Repossessed. He had called the company and told them where to find it. Still, I got dressed, called for a ride, and went to church anyway.

Later, when I used my tax refund to buy another car, he slashed my tires in the middle of the night. I woke up ready to take my kids to daycare and head to work and I was stuck. I called the police, but they said they couldn't do anything without proof. I didn't have friends. No enemies. I only knew his family.

The threats began next. Through other people, I was told he wanted me dead. That he would make it look like an accident. That he would plant a bomb in my car. I lived every day looking over my shoulder. But I still kept going then came the day I broke. I had dropped the kids off and returned home on my day off. I tried to clean. Tried to keep busy. But as I was making my bed, I collapsed to the floor.

I cried like I'd never cried before. I didn't whisper I wailed. "God, why me? Why are You letting this happen? Don't You love me?" I poured it all out, right there on the floor. And somewhere between the tears and the prayers... I fell asleep. When I woke up, the sun was shining through the window. And for the first time in a long time, I felt something I hadn't felt in months: peace. Not because the battle was over, But because God was with me in it.

I thought leaving would be the end of the pain. I didn't know it was the beginning of my becoming.

I remember thinking that once I left my abuser, everything would finally be over that I'd be able to breathe, to live again. But the moment I stepped away, life hit me harder than I ever imagined. The court temporarily gave custody of my children to my abuser until I could prove I had a stable place to live for the next hearing.

That broke me in ways I can't even put into words.

I couldn't eat. I couldn't sleep. I lost so much weight, wasting away under the pressure of grief and fear. I was still breastfeeding my baby—just seven months old—and suddenly, he was gone from my arms. It felt like someone had ripped my soul right out of my body. I was living in a nightmare that I couldn't wake up from.

I remember lying in bed, staring at the ceiling, wondering how I was still alive. Wondering how a system that was supposed to protect me could punish me. I had done the right thing. I had walked away. But somehow, I was the one paying the price.

There were days I wanted to give up. I didn't understand the court system. I didn't have a lawyer. I had no idea what to say or what paperwork to file. I was drained—emotionally, spiritually, financially. There were moments when I questioned everything... even God. I asked Him, "Where are You? Why did You let this happen?"

But even in my doubt, God was working behind the scenes.

Eventually, I scraped together enough to rent a place of my own. It wasn't perfect, but it was mine. And it was the key to seeing my babies again. I'll never forget the moment I held them after being apart. I hugged them so tight I couldn't breathe. I didn't want to let go. I had to be strong for them. I didn't want them to see me cry… but I cried myself to sleep every night.

I looked into my babies' eyes, and something rose up in me. A fire. A decision. I said to myself, *"If I don't fight for them, who will?"* They couldn't speak for themselves, and no one else was listening. I had no choice but to become their voice, their defender, their home.

I didn't have money for an attorney. So I called my sister. She was shocked. She couldn't believe this was happening in America. But she didn't ask questions—she moved into action. She found a lawyer and paid the full amount. I'll never forget what she told me: *"You'll pay me back when you have your life back."*

She had more faith in me than I had in myself. I felt like I was drowning in the deepest sea with no strength to swim, and she was the one whispering, *"You will make it."*

When I met the attorney, he asked me so many questions. Some I didn't even know how to answer. But he listened. We set a court date, and my sister drove all the way from Miami to Tallahassee just to stand by my side. I felt supported for the first time in a long time.

But the courtroom was still terrifying. My abuser stood there and lied about everything. He painted me as unstable, unfit, unworthy. I had no physical proof to fight his words. And the hardest part? I had to speak respectfully about someone who had nearly destroyed me. That was one of the hardest things I've ever done.

But God Always Wins

My abuser brought his cousin to testify against me. He even brought a woman he was flirting with to try to convince the court I was mentally unstable. They were determined to break me. To bury me in lies. But what they didn't know is that **God was already in the courtroom**.

I had no physical witness. But God became my witness.

While everyone around him lied to make me look unfit, **God was speaking truth** in the hearts of those who mattered. In the places where I had no voice, God spoke for me. I stood on His promise—even when everything in me wanted to collapse.

I eventually regained **50/50 custody** of my children. But the battle wasn't over. He was furious. He wanted full control. So he continued to torment me in other ways—ways meant to break my spirit.

At the time, I had a car, but I couldn't keep up with the payments. One Sunday morning, I opened the door to go to church—and it was gone. He had called the finance company and told them where to find it. They came and repossessed it.

Still, I pressed forward. I called someone for a ride and went to church anyway.

Then tax season came. I filed my return on my birthday in February. As soon as I got the money, I bought a used car. I thought I could finally breathe again.

But the next morning, I walked outside to find my **tires stabbed**. I couldn't take my children to school. I couldn't go to work. I called the police, filed a report... but I had no proof it was him. And without proof, they couldn't act.

He began sending threats through people I used to know. Messages like:

- *"I'll put a bomb in your car."*
- *"I'll make your death look like an accident."*

The fear was real. And yet—I kept going.

One day, I was so exhausted I could barely move. I dropped the kids at school and daycare. It was my day off. I started cleaning the house, and somewhere between straightening pillows and folding laundry, I just collapsed on the bed... and cried.

I cried until I couldn't breathe. And then I did something I hadn't done in a long time.

I **prayed.**

I prayed with every ounce of my soul. I asked God, *"Why me? Why am I still going through this? Do You even love me?"*

I prayed until I fell asleep on the floor.

When I woke up... I felt peace. A peace I hadn't felt in years. It didn't fix everything, but it reminded me: **God hadn't forgotten me.** He saw me. And He was still writing my story.

Reflection

God doesn't promise an easy road, but He promises redemption. He takes the broken pieces of your life and builds something beautiful. Even when the world tries to bury you, **He brings you back stronger**.

If you've been through the fire—if you're still walking through it—know this: **you're not alone**. God gives second chances. And when He restores, He restores better.

Chapter 2: Forgiving Him

I didn't forgive him because he deserved it—I forgave him because I deserved peace.

Forgiveness was the last thing I thought I'd ever offer to the person who broke me. After everything I went through—the lies, the court battles, the threats, the pain—I couldn't imagine letting go of the anger. I carried it like armor. I thought it was protecting me. But over time, I realized it was only imprisoning me.

I thought if I forgave him, it would mean I was weak. That I was excusing what he did. But it wasn't about him—it was about me. My freedom. My healing. My peace.

I had to forgive him... not because he apologized. He never did. Not because he changed. He didn't. I forgave him because I wanted to love myself again. Truly. Deeply. Fully. And I couldn't do that while carrying the weight of his actions.

Forgiveness was the bridge between who I had been and the woman I was becoming.

It didn't happen overnight. It came in layers. It came in prayers that started with anger and ended with surrender. It came in moments when I wanted revenge but chose release instead. I cried through it. I screamed through it. I laid it all at God's feet—and I trusted Him to do what I couldn't.

And in that release, I found something unexpected. Peace.

Not perfection. Not justice. But peace. Because forgiveness didn't make him innocent—it made me free.

"Forgiveness didn't set him free—it set me free."

I didn't forgive him because he deserved it—I forgave him because **I deserved peace**.

Forgiveness was the last thing I thought I'd ever offer to the person who broke me. After everything I went through—the lies, the court battles, the threats, the pain—I couldn't imagine letting go of the anger. I carried it like armor. I thought it was protecting me. But over time, I realized it was only **imprisoning me**.

Anger made me feel powerful, like I had something to hold onto in the chaos. But that anger was eating me alive. It was showing up in my body—headaches, sleepless nights, exhaustion. It was showing up in my spirit—I couldn't fully laugh, love, or trust. It was standing in the way of everything I wanted to become.

I used to believe that forgiving him would mean he won. That it would erase the pain or give him permission to keep hurting others. But God showed me that forgiveness **wasn't about him at all—it was about me.** My freedom. My healing. My next chapter.

He never said sorry. He never changed. He never tried to make things right. But I had to forgive him anyway. Why? Because I wanted to love myself again. Truly. Deeply. Fully. And I couldn't do that while carrying the weight of what he did.

Forgiveness was the **bridge between who I was and who I was becoming**. It was the hardest thing I've ever done—but it was also the most powerful.

What Forgiveness Is NOT

Forgiveness doesn't mean forgetting.
It doesn't mean going back.
It doesn't mean pretending it didn't happen.

Forgiveness does **not** mean reconciliation.
It means releasing your soul from the bondage of bitterness.

You can forgive and still have boundaries.
You can forgive and still protect your peace.
You can forgive and still walk away.

How I Started to Forgive

It didn't happen overnight. I didn't wake up one day and feel a wave of peace. Forgiveness came in layers. It came in moments when I could've spoken badly about him, but didn't. It came in prayers that started with, *"God, help me not hate him,"* and eventually turned into, *"God, help me release him to You."*

I prayed for the strength to forgive. I asked God to remove the weight from my chest, the poison from my thoughts. And I gave myself permission to cry, scream, write, process—all of it. Forgiveness was messy. But it was holy.

Forgiveness Gave Me Back My Power

Every time I forgave a memory, I reclaimed a piece of myself.
Every time I released a lie he told, I made room for truth.
Every time I let go of vengeance, I picked up peace.

I wasn't weak for forgiving—I was **finally free**.

I stopped replaying his words in my mind.
I stopped explaining my worth to people who didn't want to understand.
I stopped holding my breath waiting for closure from someone who was never capable of giving it.

And that? That was the moment I started breathing again. That was when my healing truly began.

Reflections for You, Beautiful Reader

If you're still holding on to the pain someone caused you, I see you.
I know what it's like to carry rage in your bones and shame in your soul.
But I also know what it's like to **finally let it go**.

Forgiveness isn't a one-time thing. It's a daily decision. Some days you'll feel strong. Some days you'll want to scream again. That's okay. Healing is not linear. But keep choosing peace.

Forgive—because your soul was not made to carry this forever.
Forgive—because you deserve to be free.
Forgive—because you are not what they did to you.
You are what God is doing in you now.

Chapter 3: Maintain Self-Care

"I had to care for the woman I'd abandoned—the one in the mirror."

After surviving so much pain, fear, and loss, I realized something no one had ever taught me: I couldn't afford to neglect myself anymore. I had spent years in survival mode, doing whatever it took to protect my children and hold everything together. But there came a moment when I looked in the mirror and saw a woman I barely recognized—tired, burned out, and invisible.

I had shown up for everyone else. Now it was time to show up for me.

Healing wasn't just about getting my children back or escaping abuse. It was about rebuilding myself—piece by piece. I wasn't just broken—I was buried. And self-care became my shovel. It was how I began to dig my way back to the surface but self-care wasn't just bubble baths and candles. It was deep. Gritty. Honest. Some days it meant saying "no." Other days it meant crying in the shower and still getting up to face the day. Self-care, for me, was the daily decision to treat myself like I mattered.

Here's how I began my journey back to wholeness:

Physical Self-Care

My body had been through war—carrying stress, trauma, exhaustion, and grief. I had ignored it for too long. I started with small steps.

Drinking water. Taking slow walks with my children. Making myself real meals instead of skipping or surviving on junk.

Some mornings, I'd play music and dance in the kitchen while I cooked. Just to remember that joy still lived somewhere inside me. I'd stretch my arms and breathe deeply as if to say, "You're safe now."

Physical self-care reminded me that my body wasn't just a vessel for survival. It was sacred. It had carried life, endured pain, and it deserved love.

Social Self-Care

I had isolated myself for so long. For years, the only people in my world were his family. After I left, I didn't know who I could trust. I was embarrassed, ashamed, afraid people wouldn't understand but I also knew I couldn't heal in isolation.

So I started small—calling my sister more, joining a women's support group, saying "yes" to conversations that felt safe. At first, it was uncomfortable. Vulnerability always is. But slowly, I began to rebuild a circle of support. Social self-care isn't about being surrounded by people—it's about finding people who make you feel seen. Who pour into you. Who remind you that you're not alone.

Mental Self-Care

My mind had been under attack for years by my abuser, the court system, trauma, and my own doubts. I had carried so many lies: "You're not enough. You'll never recover. No one will believe you." So I fought back with truth.

I started journaling. Writing down my feelings, my prayers, and even my confusion. I filled notebooks with pain and hope. I let my mind breathe. I also started listening to motivational messages, sermons, and positive content to rewire my thinking. I gave myself permission to stop replaying the past and start imagining a future.

Emotional Self-Care

This was the hardest part—because I had taught myself not to feel. I had been so used to surviving that I didn't have space to process emotions. I didn't want to cry anymore. I didn't want to feel anything that would slow me down but healing demanded honesty.

So I let myself cry in the shower. I let myself laugh with my kids, even when my heart still ached. I allowed myself to grieve, to rage, to hope. And most importantly, I stopped judging myself for feeling "too much." I learned that my emotions weren't weaknesses—they were proof that I was alive. That I hadn't gone numb. That I still had heart.

Spiritual Self-Care

Through it all, one person that never let go of me—God. Even when I questioned Him, even when I felt abandoned, I knew He was the only reason I was still breathing. Spiritual self-care became my anchor. I started praying not out of habit, but from my heart. I didn't always have the right words. Sometimes I just sat in silence and cried. But God heard it all.

I read scriptures about restoration and promises. I listened to worship even when I didn't feel worthy. I let the presence of God become my safe space again because when the world is unstable, the soul needs something unshakable.

You deserve to be whole.

Self-care after trauma isn't pretty. It's not about luxury. It's about survival. It's about rebirth. You can't pour into your children, your healing, your future if you're running on empty.

So give yourself permission:

To rest.

To feel.

To be.

To heal.

Because the woman inside you? She's still there. And she's worthy of every ounce of love you've ever given to everyone else.

Chapter 4: Spiritual Beauty

"The glow they saw on me wasn't makeup. It was mercy."

There is a kind of beauty this world can't explain. It's not the beauty of curves, clothes, or curled eyelashes. It's the beauty that lingers in your presence. It's how your eyes shine after they've cried for months. It's the grace in your voice when you have every reason to be bitter.

That kind of beauty is spiritual. And it's powerful.

After walking through trauma, shame, betrayal, and abandonment, I thought I would never feel beautiful again. My confidence was broken. My body was tired. My soul was weary. But as I began to heal, I discovered something that changed me forever:

Spiritual beauty doesn't come from perfection. It comes from surrender.

It comes from opening your heart to God and allowing Him to restore what pain tried to destroy. It shows up in how you walk through life— not because everything is easy, but because you know Who holds you together.

Grooming the Soul

We groom our outer appearance all the time—fix our hair, polish our nails, apply makeup. But after trauma, our soul is what needs grooming the most. Mine was dry. Bitter in some places. Weak in others. There were parts of me I had buried so deeply, I forgot they existed.

So I made a decision: I would care for my soul the way I once cared for my appearance.

That looked like fasting not just from food, but from distractions. That looked like journaling my prayers, worshiping through tears, and letting go of old music, habits, and people that drained me.

It was a slow, intentional pruning. Every time I forgave someone—even if they didn't deserve it I was trimming away resentment. Every time I chose peace over pettiness, I was watering my roots.

Spiritual beauty comes from within, but it doesn't happen by accident. It's a practice. A lifestyle. A devotion to becoming more whole than we were yesterday.

Healing isn't just about what you fix on the outside—it's about caring for the parts of you no one else sees.

I had to look at my soul like a garden. Some areas were dry. Some were tangled in resentment. Some were bruised by shame I didn't ask for. But God didn't leave me there.

I began **grooming my soul** the way I would groom my hair or skin. I started with what I consumed—scriptures, worship, peace. I removed what was toxic—fearful thoughts, comparison, bitterness. I fasted. I journaled. I forgave. I let God tend to the soil of my heart.

Every act of spiritual self-care was like watering a seed inside me. And slowly, my soul began to bloom.

Soul Searching

Healing forced me to ask hard questions:

• Who am I when no one is looking?

• What do I believe?

• What breaks me? What heals me?

• What does God say about me?

These weren't surface-level reflections. They were deep. They required honesty. I had to stop living based on who others said I was and ask God to reintroduce me to the woman He created.

I discovered I was not weak—I was resilient.

I wasn't too emotional—I was deeply compassionate.

I wasn't broken beyond repair—I was being rebuilt with purpose.

There was a time I looked in the mirror and didn't know who I was.

I had spent so long surviving that I forgot what it meant to actually live.

I asked myself:

- Who am I without the pain?
- What do I love—really love?
- Who is the woman God says I am?

It took time. And it took truth. I stopped looking for outside approval. I stopped comparing my journey to others. I stopped defining myself by my past.

And I started listening to **God's voice** over the noise of the world. He told me:

"You are fearfully and wonderfully made."
"You are my daughter."
"You are chosen. Worthy. Seen."

Soul searching helped me **find the woman buried beneath survival**. And what I found was beautiful.

Determining Right from Wrong

Abuse confuses the lines. When you're manipulated long enough, you start to question your own instincts. I used to feel guilty for setting boundaries, like I was being selfish for protecting my peace. But through healing, I learned:

Healthy love doesn't silence you.

It doesn't control you.

It doesn't make you question your worth.

God began to restore my discernment. I started praying, "God, if it's not from You, don't let it stay in my life." I asked for wisdom to see red flags early, to walk away when necessary, and to stop begging for what was hurting me.

Part of spiritual beauty is clarity. Seeing clearly what is light and what is darkness—and having the strength to choose the light, even when it's lonely.

Abuse distorts reality. I questioned my instincts. I second-guessed myself. I didn't know what "normal" was anymore. But through faith and healing, I began to rebuild my inner compass.

I learned that love does not hurt.
That control is not protection.
That silence is not peace.

I had to **relearn what God says is true**, and unlearn what my trauma had taught me.

His truth became my guide:

Love is patient. Love is kind. Love does not dishonor others. (1 Corinthians 13)

I realized I had accepted things that were never okay—and I forgave myself for not knowing better. I gave myself permission to grow without shame.

Taking a Spiritual Inventory

As I healed, I sat down and asked myself some real questions:

• Where am I still hurting?

• What part of me is still holding on to shame?

• Where am I pretending to be okay when I'm not?

• What does God want to heal in me next?

This wasn't about self-judgment. It was about self-awareness. God can only heal what we're willing to reveal. So I laid it all at His feet—my fears, my doubts, my trauma, my pride, my pain and every time I gave Him another broken piece, He gave me back peace.

I got honest with God and with myself.

I asked:

- Where am I still wounded?
- Where have I stopped trusting Him?
- What needs to be surrendered?

I wrote it all down. I prayed through it. I repented. I released. And most of all—I invited God in.

Taking inventory wasn't about judging myself. It was about healing myself. One piece at a time. One truth at a time.

The Beauty They Can't Take From You

There's a beauty you carry now that no one can steal. It comes from surviving. From surrender. From knowing that you are held by something greater than yourself.

Spiritual beauty makes you glow in a storm.

It makes you speak life when you've tasted death.

It makes you walk like you know heaven is backing you up.

You don't have to wait for your life to be perfect to be spiritually beautiful.

You just have to say yes to the process.

Because every time you choose healing, forgiveness, grace, worship, or truth,

you become more radiant than before and that is the glow of a woman who knows God for herself.

"She is clothed in strength and dignity, and she laughs without fear of the future." – Proverbs 31:25

The world teaches us that beauty is on the surface. It tells us we have to look a certain way, dress a certain way, smile a certain way to be seen and valued.

But after walking through the fire of abuse, rejection, and healing, I realized something sacred:

True beauty has nothing to do with appearance—it lives in the soul.

There's something powerful about a woman who has survived what was meant to destroy her and still wakes up with grace in her spirit. That's spiritual beauty. It's not something you can buy. It's something you build—with faith, tears, and truth.

Spiritual beauty is the glow that doesn't fade.
It's the light in your eyes after you've cried through the night.
It's the strength in your smile when you've lost everything—but still choose to rise.

You don't have to be perfect to be spiritually beautiful. You just have to be open.
Open to God.
Open to healing.
Open to the woman you're becoming.

And when that inner beauty shines, **it draws the right people, opportunities, and peace** into your life.

You don't chase anything anymore—**you attract everything aligned with your spirit.**

Chapter 5: Inner Beauty

"The strongest version of me didn't show up when things were easy—it rose from the ashes."

There's a kind of beauty that no mirror can show you. No filter can capture it. No opinion can define it. It doesn't live on your skin—it lives in your soul.

That's inner beauty.

The kind that blossoms after pain.

The kind that survives betrayal and still chooses kindness.

The kind that doesn't beg to be seen, but shines quietly through how you carry yourself.

When I first started my healing journey, I thought I had to rebuild my outer life first—get a job, fix my finances, stabilize everything around me. But I soon learned the most important rebuilding had to happen within.

Because the truth is: I had been made to feel invisible for so long that I forgot I had value without anyone else's validation. I forgot I was whole before the world told me I was broken.

So I began to search—not for what made me look beautiful, but for what made me feel beautiful. Not for applause, but for alignment with the woman God created me to be.

"She is more precious than rubies. Nothing you desire can compare with her." – Proverbs 3:15

There's a kind of beauty that can't be seen at first glance.
It's not defined by makeup, fashion, or filters.
It's the kind of beauty that comes from rising after being broken.

That's inner beauty.

It's the kind of beauty that shows up in the way you love, in the way you heal, in the way you keep choosing joy when you've been surrounded by sorrow. It's quiet. It's strong. It's sacred.

Independence

I had to relearn how to live on my own. After years of being controlled, manipulated, and silenced, I had to figure out what it meant to make decisions for myself again.

It wasn't just about paying bills or managing schedules. It was about learning to trust my own voice. To say "yes" without fear. To say "no" without guilt.

I started small—applying for things on my own, organizing my home the way I liked, even choosing what to eat without asking permission. These may sound simple, but when you've lived in someone else's shadow, freedom feels revolutionary.

Independence isn't just about doing life alone—it's about being anchored in your own identity, so no one can take it from you again.

After years of control and fear, I had to **relearn how to stand on my own**.

I didn't just need to be physically free—I needed to be emotionally and spiritually free too. I had to make decisions for myself. I had to trust myself again. I had to believe that I was capable.

At first, I was scared. I second-guessed everything. But with every small step—paying bills, showing up for work, setting boundaries—I was reclaiming ground that once belonged to someone else.

Independence doesn't mean you have to do life alone. It means you get to choose **who walks with you**. It means your voice matters. It means your life is **your own**.

Confidence

Confidence didn't come back all at once. It came in whispers. In the way I stood a little taller in public. In how I answered the phone without fear. In how I looked in the mirror and started seeing myself instead of the lies he used to speak over me.

I reminded myself daily: I am fearfully and wonderfully made. I am not what I've been through. I am who God says I am.

Every time I showed up to work, smiled at my kids, or walked into a room I once would've avoided, I was choosing confidence. I was saying, "I deserve to be here."

Not because I'm perfect but because I'm enough.

I used to avoid the mirror because it echoed the lies I had been told.

I had been called ugly. Weak. Too much. Not enough.
But healing taught me that confidence isn't loud—it's **rooted**.
It's not about being better than anyone else—it's about being true to yourself.

I began speaking life to the woman I saw.
"You are beautiful."
"You are strong."
"You are worthy."

Even when I didn't believe it yet, I kept speaking it. And something in me began to change. My posture changed. My energy changed. My words changed. And slowly… **I changed.**

Confidence grew as I set boundaries.
Confidence grew as I told the truth.
Confidence grew every time I chose me.

Integrity

One of the most powerful lessons I learned was this:

Just because someone wronged you doesn't mean you have to lose yourself to fight back.

My abuser lied. Manipulated. Tried to destroy my character in court and in the community. But I refused to meet him on that level. Not because I was weak but because I was rooted.

I chose to take the high road—not out of fear, but out of strength.

I stayed true to who I was.

I spoke the truth, even when it hurt.

I honored God in private, not just in public.

Integrity is choosing peace over pride.

It's staying grounded when life tries to shake you.

It's knowing you don't have to lower your standard to win—because God defends the righteous.

Abuse tried to make me bitter, but God kept my heart soft.

My abuser lied on the stand. He twisted stories. He manipulated others to make himself look like the victim. And I could've done the same. But I chose integrity.

It wasn't easy. It wasn't fair. But I knew that **my character mattered more than his lies**.

Integrity is doing what's right even when no one is watching.
Even when you're angry.
Even when you're tired.
Even when it would be easier to play dirty.

I chose to take the high road—not because I was weak, but because I knew **God would fight for me**.

My inner beauty was protected by truth.

Passion for Helping Others

My pain gave birth to purpose.

As I began to heal, I started feeling a tug on my heart—not just to survive for myself, but to reach back and help others climb out of the same pit. I wanted women who had been silenced to find their voices. I wanted mothers to know they didn't fail just because they broke. I wanted survivors to know:

"You're not crazy. You're not weak. And you are not alone."

I didn't need a stage or a spotlight. I just needed a heart willing to share. To encourage. To tell the truth because when we turn our pain into purpose, we become healers too.

When I came through the other side of my storm, I knew I couldn't keep quiet.

God didn't rescue me just so I could move on quietly.
He rescued me so I could **reach back**.

I began speaking up—not just for me, but for every woman who still thinks she's alone. I began writing, sharing, praying, encouraging. I wanted to turn my pain into purpose.

That's part of my inner beauty too:
The fire to use my voice.
The compassion to lift others.
The calling to help women rise from the ashes.

Because when you've been through hell and made it out, you don't just survive—you lead others through the smoke.

Your Inner Beauty Is Your Superpower

You don't need approval to be powerful.

You don't need perfection to be beautiful.

You don't need to wear strength like armor—you can wear it like grace.

Inner beauty is your superpower.
It's the light you carry.

The peace you protect.
The truth you walk in.
The grace you offer.
The strength you radiate—without needing to prove it to anyone.

And when that beauty blooms, **everything around you starts to shift**.

You become magnetic. Not because of your appearance, but because of your **spirit**.

You don't need to chase love.
You don't need to beg for respect.
You don't need to shrink to fit anyone's box.

You are a woman becoming.
And your inner beauty will take you places outer beauty never could.

Inner beauty is the way you keep showing up with love, even when life tries to harden you.

It's the softness you've kept, the light you've nurtured, the wisdom you carry.

It's the way you walk into a room and bring peace, not noise.

Let the world see it.

Let your children learn from it.

Let your healing speak louder than your history.

Because you—the real you—is the most beautiful part of your story.

Chapter 6: Self-Love

"I didn't wait for someone else to choose me—I chose myself."

There was a time I believed love had to come from someone else to be real. I thought I had to earn it. That I had to be quiet, small, pleasing, or perfect to be loved. But after everything I went through—losing myself, losing my peace, almost losing my life—I came to understand one life-changing truth:

The greatest love story I'll ever live is the one I have with myself.

It wasn't always easy to get there. I had to unlearn a lot of things. I had to heal the version of me that begged for scraps. I had to forgive the woman I once was—not because she was wrong, but because she didn't know any better.

Self-love wasn't a trend or a hashtag.

It was a rescue mission.

It was the slow, intentional, spiritual journey of remembering who I was before trauma made me forget.

"Love your neighbor as yourself." – Mark 12:31
But how can we love anyone well… if we don't love ourselves first?

For so long, I thought love was something I had to earn.
I believed I had to be needed to feel valuable. I thought love meant
sacrifice—even if it meant losing myself in the process.

But the truth is—**self-love is the foundation of every healthy thing**
that will ever grow in your life.

And for me, it started in the ruins.
It started when I had nothing left but my reflection and my breath.
It started when I chose to stop asking, *"What's wrong with me?"* and
instead started whispering, *"What's beautiful about me?"*

Falling in Love with Myself

I remember the day I looked in the mirror and didn't recognize the
woman staring back at me. Her eyes looked tired. Her spirit dim. But
underneath the pain, I could still see something: a flicker. A glimpse of
the woman God always knew I could be.

That day, I made a promise to myself:

"I will no longer abandon you."

I started doing small things to show myself love.

I wrote notes to myself.

I bought myself flowers.

I spoke kindly in my mind instead of criticizing my reflection.

Even when I didn't believe the words yet, I said them until I did:

"You are worthy. You are beautiful. You are enough."

Falling in love with myself didn't mean I stopped loving others—it meant I finally had enough love to give without breaking.

There was a time I looked in the mirror and didn't even recognize myself.

I saw sadness in my eyes.
I saw trauma in my skin.
I saw weariness in my posture.

But I also saw **a woman who didn't quit**.

I saw a mother who kept showing up.
I saw a survivor who made it through storms.
I saw a daughter of God whose story wasn't over.

That's when I began to fall in love—with myself.

Not with perfection. Not with performance. But with **presence**.

I started celebrating my softness. My boldness. My emotions. My strength.
I started being gentle with myself when I messed up. I let go of the guilt. I released the pressure. I replaced judgment with grace.

I began speaking to myself the way I spoke to people I loved:
"You're doing your best."
"You've come so far."
"You are worthy of good things."

And over time, I started to believe it.

Loving My Children from a Place of Wholeness

My children were always my why. In the darkest times, they were my light. But as I started healing, I realized I couldn't just love them from a place of survival. I needed to love them from a place of wholeness.

I began to see how my healing helped them feel safe.

How my laughter gave them permission to laugh.

How my peace created peace for them.

They watched me rebuild, and through that, I taught them strength without even using words.

I showed them that love is not pain.

Love is presence.

Love is truth.

Love is showing up—even when you're tired, even when you're scared, even when the world told you to quit.

My children were the mirror that reflected my growth.

They saw me cry, but they also saw me rise.
They heard my prayers. They felt my love.
They watched me walk away from what was killing me—and that became their example of strength.

Loving my children meant giving them a healed version of me.

I didn't want them to inherit my wounds. I wanted them to inherit **my wisdom**.

I had to teach them, not just through words, but through how I lived.
So I chose to love myself in front of them:
By setting boundaries.
By resting without guilt.
By choosing joy even on hard days.

I taught them that loving yourself is not selfish—it's a survival skill.
And because I loved me, I could love them **fully, freely, fiercely.**

Loving My Family with Boundaries and Grace

Healing also changed how I loved my family. It taught me that love doesn't mean endless access. It doesn't mean tolerating pain for the sake of blood. It means truth. It means boundaries. It means freedom.

My sister stood beside me when I had no strength left. She believed in me, invested in me, and reminded me I was not alone. And through that love, I found the courage to rise.

But I also learned how to protect my peace—even from those I love. I learned that love and boundaries can exist in the same space. And I learned that when I love myself well, I love others better—because I'm not giving from a place of emptiness, but from overflow.

Family can be complicated. Some support you. Some stay silent. Some hurt you. And some save you.

Through this journey, I learned to love my family from a place of **wholeness**.
Not obligation. Not guilt. Not shame. But truth.

My sister showed me love that restored my faith in people. She saw the broken pieces of my life and said, *"I believe in you anyway."*
That's love. That's family.

But I also had to learn that **loving someone doesn't mean letting them have access to you**.
I had to set boundaries. I had to guard my peace. I had to say no. And I had to be okay with that.

Loving my family now looks like:

- Speaking the truth in love
- Showing up when I'm whole, not when I'm empty
- Giving grace—but not enabling

Self-love gave me the strength to **love others from overflow**, not depletion.

Self-Love Is Not Selfish—It's Sacred

You were never meant to love from your wounds.

You were meant to love from your worth.

That means resting when you need to.

Walking away when it's toxic.

Speaking up when it's hard.

And never apologizing for choosing yourself.

Self-love is how we honor the God who created us.

It's not arrogance.
It's not selfishness.
It's not putting others down to feel better.

Self-love is:

- Resting when you're tired
- Saying no when it's not right
- Celebrating yourself without waiting for permission
- Protecting your energy
- Believing God made no mistake when He created you

It's understanding that your value doesn't change depending on who's around you.
You are valuable *because you exist*.

Reflection

Self-love is your birthright.

Not something you earn.
Not something someone else gives you.
It's yours.

And when you walk in that love, you **attract better, choose better, and become better**.

You love your children better.
You love your partner better.
You love your purpose better.

Because when you love yourself, you don't settle.
You don't chase.
You don't shrink.

You rise.

It's how we say, "Thank You for making me. I won't treat Your creation like it's disposable."

A Prayer for the Woman Learning to Love Herself Again

God, teach me to see myself the way You see me.

Help me forgive the woman I was and make room for the woman I'm becoming.

Heal the places where I feel unworthy.

Silence the lies I've believed about my value.

Give me strength to stand, softness to feel, and grace to grow.

Let my life be proof that love starts with You—and flows through me.

Amen.

Chapter 7: Marriage

"Love is not meant to break you—it's meant to build you."

Before healing, I thought love had to come with pain.

I thought that being chosen meant being needed... even if that need drained me.

I thought love was supposed to hurt, and that if I just loved harder, maybe it would get better.

But pain was never the proof of love.

Sacrifice was never meant to be one-sided.

And love? Real love—the kind that honors your soul—is nothing like abuse.

God showed me that love is gentle.

It is kind.

It tells the truth.

It gives space to breathe, to grow, to become.

"He who finds a wife finds a good thing and obtains favor from the Lord." – Proverbs 18:22

I used to think love was supposed to hurt.
I thought if someone needed me, it meant they loved me.
I believed that if I sacrificed enough, cried enough, stayed quiet enough, I would be loved back.

But now I know the truth:
Real love doesn't break you—it builds you.

Marriage isn't about completing someone. It's not about fixing someone.
It's about **choosing** someone, every day, from a place of wholeness—not woundedness.

An Angelic Husband

I never imagined I could trust someone again.

I had built so many walls that love would have to knock down every brick just to reach me. But then God sent a man who didn't come to tear down walls—he came to sit beside them, patiently, until I felt safe enough to let him in.

He didn't try to fix me.

He didn't rush my healing.

He didn't make me feel like a burden.

Instead, he prayed with me.

He honored my story.

He covered me in love and peace.

When I woke up with anxiety, he held my hand and said, "You're safe now."

When I doubted myself, he reminded me, "You are strong. You are whole. You are mine."

This is what love is supposed to feel like:

Peaceful. Powerful. Protective. Present.

It's not that he was perfect. It's that he was real.

And I didn't have to shrink, soften, or silence myself to be loved by him.

He saw me—fully—and chose me anyway.

When God brought my husband into my life, I wasn't sure I was ready.

I had scars. I had triggers. I had walls.
But he never tried to tear them down—he waited for me to open the door.

He didn't rush me.
He didn't push me.
He didn't judge me.

Instead, he covered me in prayer.
He listened without interrupting.
He spoke life over me in places where I had only heard lies.

He didn't need me to shrink—he gave me space to expand.
He didn't need me to be perfect—he loved the parts I was still healing.

This is what love looks like after abuse:
It's soft.
It's steady.
It's sacred.

He became a reminder that **God doesn't just rescue—He restores**.

Love from My Children

My babies have always been my lifeline. But now, as I've healed, I get to experience a different kind of love with them. I get to show up fully—not just as a mother, but as a woman who is whole.

They've seen me cry.

They've watched me fight.

And now, they watch me glow.

They hug me tighter.

They laugh more freely.

They say "I love you" and "I'm proud of you," because they feel what healing has created in our home.

My children were there for the storm. They felt it.
They cried with me.
They held my hand when I was shaking.
They watched the door, waiting to see if I was okay.

So when they saw me in a peaceful, joyful marriage—**they healed too.**

They learned that love doesn't scream.
Love doesn't threaten.
Love doesn't destroy.

They saw how a man treats a woman when he is submitted to God.
They saw how prayer fills a home.
They saw that laughter can replace fear, and kindness can replace control.

Their hugs are tighter now.
Their "I love yous" are more frequent.
Their hearts are more open.

Because when I healed, **they healed too**.

Our bond is sacred. Not because it's perfect, but because it's real.

We survived the storm together. And now, we're living in the peace I prayed for.

The Power of Respect

Respect is more than politeness—it's a deep understanding of who someone is and what they carry. I used to beg for it. Now, I embody it.

My husband respects me not because of what I do for him, but because of who I am.

My children respect me not because I demand it, but because they've watched me rise with dignity and grace.

And most importantly—I respect myself.

I no longer tolerate chaos to feel wanted.

I no longer play small to make others comfortable.

I no longer stay silent when I need to speak.

There's a quiet power in knowing your worth—and not needing anyone else to confirm it.

Respect is the foundation of real love.
And that starts with **self-respect**.

I had to teach the world how to treat me by first treating myself with love, dignity, and truth.

Now:

- I walk with my head held high
- I speak with purpose, not fear
- I choose peace over people-pleasing
- I say no without guilt and yes without fear

My husband respects me because he knows what I've walked through.
My children respect me because they've seen me rise from the ashes.
And most importantly—I respect myself.

Respect is not demanded.
It's radiated.

You Deserve This Kind of Love

You deserve love that makes you feel safe.

Love that adds to your life—not takes from it.

Love that lets you breathe, that sees you clearly, that honors your journey.

Don't settle for a love that needs your silence to survive.

Wait for the love that welcomes your voice, your vision, your vulnerability.

Because it does exist.

And you are already worthy of it.

A Message for You, Sister

If you're wondering if you'll ever love again...
If you're afraid that your heart is too broken...
If you think no one will ever see you as whole again...

Hear me clearly:

You are not too much.
You are not too broken.
You are not too late.

The right love will not rush your healing.
The right love will make room for your growth.
The right love will honor your journey—not minimize it.

You don't need to beg for it.
You don't need to perform for it.
You don't need to lose yourself to keep it.

You are the blessing.
And when God sends the one—he'll know it.

Scripture to Hold On To

1 Timothy 4:12

"Don't let anyone look down on you because you are young, but set an example for the believers in speech, in conduct, in love, in faith and in purity."

Let your life be an example. Let your love be a testimony. Let your healing be loud.

You are not just a survivor.

You are a wife, a mother, a warrior, a woman of faith.

You are not just a survivor. You are a testimony.
You are not just healing—you are living.
You are not just waiting for love—you are walking in it.

Real love exists.
And yes—you can love again.
And be loved well.

I have loved again.
I have forgiven.
I have healed.
And I am free.

Chapter 8: The Woman in the Mirror

"But we all, with unveiled face, beholding as in a mirror the glory of the Lord, are being transformed..." – 2 Corinthians 3:18

There was a time I couldn't even look in the mirror.

Not because I hated what I saw, but because I didn't recognize her.
The woman staring back at me looked tired. Worn down. Lost.
She had given so much away—her voice, her light, her peace—that it felt like there was barely anything left.

But little by little, piece by piece, I started to meet her again.
Not the version shaped by someone else's lies.
Not the woman who shrank herself to survive.
But the real me—the one God always saw.

Abuse Strips You of Your Identity

When you're in survival mode, you don't have time to be soft, curious, creative, or free.
You're too busy protecting yourself.
Too busy making sure no one gets mad.
Too busy trying not to say the wrong thing.

Over time, I lost sight of who I was.
I became what he wanted: quiet, small, compliant, apologetic.
I stopped dreaming.
I stopped laughing from my belly.
I stopped trusting myself.

And when I finally escaped the abuse, I still carried his voice inside my head.

"You're nothing without me."
"No one else will ever love you."
"You'll never make it on your own."

Those lies echoed... until I replaced them with truth.

Meeting Myself Again

I started small.
I looked in the mirror—really looked—and said:
"You are not broken. You are becoming."
"You are still here. You are still worthy."
"You are beautiful—not because you're flawless, but because you're alive."

I stopped avoiding my reflection. I began caring for my body—not to impress anyone, but to honor myself. I wore what made me feel radiant. I smiled just because I felt light inside me again.

And more than anything... I listened.

I listened to my laughter.
I listened to my silence.
I listened to the voice I had buried beneath fear.

Redefining Myself by God's Truth

The most powerful thing I ever did was stop letting someone else's opinion define me.

Instead, I asked God, *"Who do You say I am?"*

And He answered:

"You are fearfully and wonderfully made." (Psalm 139:14)
"You are chosen."
"You are redeemed."
"You are not what they did—you are what I'm doing."

God showed me that my identity wasn't something I had to create—it was something I had to **come back to**.

I was always His daughter.
I was always a light-bearer.
I was always a force, even when I felt invisible.

Becoming the Woman I Was Always Meant to Be

Now, when I look in the mirror, I see more than a survivor.

I see a warrior.
A mother.
A truth-teller.
A nurturer.
A leader.
A woman who said, *"This ends with me,"* and meant it.

I don't need the world to validate me.
I don't need a relationship to complete me.
I don't need approval to feel seen.

I see myself.
And because I love what I see—I protect her.

Question

Who is the woman in your mirror?

Not the one shaped by trauma.
Not the one forced to smile while breaking.
Not the one others labeled.

But the one who is finally… free.

Look into your own eyes today and remind yourself:

"I am still here. I am still whole. And I am finally coming home to me.

Chapter 9: Rebuilding My Voice

"She opens her mouth with wisdom, and the teaching of kindness is on her tongue." – Proverbs 31:26

When I was in the relationship, I lost my voice.

Not because I didn't have one—but because it was **silenced**.
Every time I tried to speak, I was met with criticism, threats, or manipulation.
Every time I had a thought or opinion, I was made to feel small or wrong.
So eventually... I stopped speaking.

I learned to keep quiet to avoid conflict.
I learned to smile so no one would ask questions.
I learned to say "I'm okay" when I wasn't—even when I was breaking.

But silence didn't protect me.
It just buried me.

Abuse Shatters Confidence

People think losing your voice means being soft-spoken or shy. But for survivors, it's deeper.

Losing your voice means:

- You doubt your truth
- You apologize for existing
- You second-guess every word before it leaves your mouth
- You fear being misunderstood, dismissed, or punished

I had internalized so many lies about who I was that I didn't know how to speak up for myself—even after I left.

But healing... healing taught me how to **rebuild** my voice from the inside out.

Step by Step, I Took It Back

Rebuilding my voice wasn't loud at first. It was **quiet and sacred.**

It started with journaling.
Then speaking up in prayer.
Then telling my story—to God, to myself, to trusted people.
Then saying "no" without explaining.
Then saying "yes" to what aligned with my healing.

I remember the first time I disagreed with someone and didn't feel afraid.
I remember the first time I told someone, *"This is not okay,"* and didn't shrink afterward.
I remember the first time I looked someone in the eye and said, *"I deserve better."*

Every moment I used my voice—I reclaimed power I didn't even know I had lost.

Boundaries Are a Form of Speaking

Using my voice didn't always mean words.
Sometimes, it was in my actions.
Sometimes, it was in walking away.
Sometimes, it was in choosing silence when I used to argue to be heard.

I learned that **boundaries are sacred conversations**. They say:

- "I love myself enough to say no."
- "I'm not available for disrespect."
- "I'm not explaining my worth anymore."

My voice became the gatekeeper of my peace.

Telling My Story Became My Superpower

What once shamed me now empowers me.

The things I was too afraid to speak about?
They became the very stories that healed others.

I started sharing—not just the pain, but the lessons.
Not just the trauma, but the triumph.
Not just the fear, but the **faith** that pulled me through.

And every time another woman said, *"Me too…"*
I knew: **my voice matters**.

A Voice That Now Speaks Life

Now, my voice is not just loud—it's **anointed**.
It speaks love into my children.
It sets the tone for my home.
It rebukes what's toxic and calls in what's holy.
It speaks to mountains and tells them to move.

My voice is no longer something I fear—it's something I thank God for.

And if I had to walk through fire to find it…
So be it.

Questions

To the woman reading this—your voice still lives in you.

Even if it's faint.
Even if it trembles.
Even if it feels lost under years of silence.

Your voice is not gone—it's waiting.

Start with a whisper.
Start with a prayer.
Start by telling your truth to yourself.
And then... speak.

Because **your voice is a weapon, a light, a song, and a story**.
And the world needs to hear it.

Chapter 10: The Power of Prayer

"The earnest prayer of a righteous person has great power and produces wonderful results." – James 5:16 (NLT)

If there's one thing that never left me through it all—it was **prayer**.

There were days I couldn't speak to anyone.
Days I couldn't stop crying.
Days I felt like no one understood.
But even in those moments, I could still **talk to God**.

And that's what saved me.

I Prayed Through the Pain

I didn't grow up knowing how to pray like the church mothers.
I didn't have fancy words or perfect scriptures memorized.
But I had pain.
And I had a heart that needed help.

And that was enough.

Some prayers were whispered through tears.
Some were shouted into the darkness.
Some were silent cries with no words—just the ache of my soul reaching out.

I prayed when I had nothing left.
When my car was taken.
When my children were gone.
When my name was being slandered.
When fear told me I'd never make it.

And somehow… God always answered.
Not always immediately. Not always how I expected.
But He always showed up.

Prayer Was My Protection

There were things I survived that I *know* were because of prayer.

I believe prayer covered me when I was being followed.
I believe prayer blocked attacks that were being planned behind my back.
I believe prayer changed the minds of judges, softened hearts, and exposed lies.
I believe prayer kept me alive.

Even when the police didn't believe me… God did.
Even when the court was against me… God wasn't.
Even when I had no physical proof… my prayers became my evidence.

Prayer Became My Weapon

At first, I prayed out of desperation.
But then I started praying out of **authority**.

I realized I didn't have to beg God—I could stand on His promises.
So I began to declare:

- "No weapon formed against me shall prosper." (Isaiah 54:17)
- "I am the head and not the tail." (Deuteronomy 28:13)
- "God will fight for me." (Exodus 14:14)
- "He makes a way where there is no way." (Isaiah 43:16)

My prayers shifted.
They became bold.

They became strategic.
They became declarations of war against the lies of the enemy.

I didn't just pray *about* my circumstances—I prayed **through** them.

More than anything, prayer changed *me*.

It gave me peace when I couldn't fix the problem.
It gave me hope when I couldn't see a way out.
It reminded me that I wasn't doing life alone.

Prayer helped me forgive.
Prayer helped me stay calm in court.
Prayer helped me get out of bed when I wanted to give up.

It wasn't just about God fixing things.
It was about **God fixing me**—strengthening me, healing me, rebuilding me.

If you feel like no one is listening—pray anyway.
If you don't know what to say—pray anyway.
If you're tired, angry, afraid—pray anyway.

Because **God hears you**.

And where prayer exists, **power is released**.

You don't have to be perfect to pray.
You just have to be honest.

God meets you in the mess.
He sits with you in the silence.
And He answers in ways that *no one else can.*

So don't stop praying.
Your miracle might be one prayer away.

Chapter 11: Raising Healed Children

"Train up a child in the way he should go; even when he is old he will not depart from it." – Proverbs 22:6

There is no manual for how to raise children after you've survived abuse.
No one teaches you how to rebuild a home after it's been broken.
No one prepares you for the fear that the pain you endured might follow your children.

But I knew one thing for sure:
The cycle had to stop with me.

They Were There for the Storm

My babies didn't ask to be part of the battle.
But they were there.
They heard the yelling.
They saw the fear in my eyes.
They watched me cry in silence.
They felt the weight I carried in my spirit.

And even though they were young, they knew.
Children always know.

That's why I made a promise to God—and to them:
"I will not just survive. I will raise you in love, not fear. In truth, not lies. In peace, not chaos."

Rebuilding Our Home With Intention

After I left, I didn't just want to be free.
I wanted to raise **free children**.

So I began creating a new atmosphere.
I filled our home with worship music and laughter.
I prayed out loud so they'd know Who we trust.
I hugged them longer.
I listened deeper.
I became emotionally available—*even when I was exhausted.*

We didn't have everything.
But we had peace.
And that became the foundation of our healing.

Teaching Them What Love Really Means

My children saw both love and dysfunction.
They needed to learn how to tell the difference.

So I began **teaching them what love is**:

- Love is gentle, not controlling.
- Love listens, it doesn't intimidate.
- Love says "I'm sorry."
- Love creates safety, not silence.

I apologized when I was wrong.
I explained why I had boundaries.
I taught them how to use their voice, even if it shook.
I reminded them daily: *"Your feelings matter. You matter."*

Breaking Generational Patterns

Just because abuse ran in my family doesn't mean it had to continue.

I stopped saying, *"That's just how things are."*
And I started saying, *"This is where it ends."*

That meant:

- Letting go of toxic traditions
- Not allowing screaming to be normal
- Modeling what healthy correction looks like
- Teaching emotional intelligence and spiritual awareness

I wasn't just raising children—I was **raising history-makers**.

Allowing Myself to Heal Alongside Them

There were moments I felt like I had to be perfect for them.
But I realized: *they don't need a perfect mom—they need a present one.*

So I let them see my healing.

I told them, *"Mommy's learning too."*
I shared parts of my story in age-appropriate ways.
I let them pray with me.
And most of all—I let them see me rest.

When I healed out loud, I gave them permission to **grow without shame**.

Reflection

Raising healed children isn't about pretending you've never been broken.
It's about showing them what **rising** looks like.

You may not have had an example growing up—but you get to become one.

Every hug you give, every truth you speak, every safe boundary you hold…
it matters.

You are not just raising children. You are raising healed generations.

And that, mama, is holy work.

Chapter 12: When Peace Feels Foreign

"The Lord gives strength to his people; the Lord blesses his people with peace." – Psalm 29:11

No one tells you how strange peace can feel when all you've ever known is survival.

I used to pray for peace.
I begged God to make the chaos stop.
I longed for a home without yelling… a life without fear… a love without pain.

But when it finally came?
When the storm calmed, the silence felt… **uncomfortable**.

Because I didn't know who I was without the fight.

I Was Addicted to Chaos and Didn't Know It

When you've been living in survival mode, your body and mind adjust to constant stress.
Your heart is always racing.
Your brain is always preparing for the next attack.
Even when it's quiet—you don't feel safe.

So when things finally settled, I wasn't relieved at first…
I was anxious.

- I didn't trust the silence.
- I didn't believe peace could last.
- I kept waiting for something bad to happen.
- I sabotaged joy because it felt unfamiliar.

Peace felt like a stranger.
And part of me missed the noise—not because it was good, but because it was **what I knew**.

Healing Meant Rewiring My Mind

I had to learn that peace wasn't boring.
It wasn't dangerous.
It wasn't a trap.

It was **sacred.**

I started speaking peace over myself:

"I am safe now."
"I deserve to rest."
"Nothing has to be falling apart for me to be valuable."

I reminded myself that I didn't have to perform.
I didn't have to explain.
I didn't have to defend my peace to anyone.

Peace is my promise—not my punishment.

Resting Without Guilt

There was a time I felt guilty for resting.

If the house was quiet, I felt like I was being lazy.
If no one was mad at me, I thought something was wrong.
If I was happy, I braced for something to steal it.

But then God whispered to my spirit:

"You don't have to earn peace. You are my daughter. I give it freely."

So I began practicing peace like a habit:

- I drank tea in silence.
- I walked barefoot on the grass.
- I lit candles and read books with no interruptions.
- I learned to enjoy my own company.

And little by little, I stopped fearing peace—and started living in it.

Embracing the Stillness

I discovered something beautiful:

Peace doesn't mean life is perfect.
It means I'm anchored when things around me are not.

Now, I don't chase chaos.
I don't overcommit.
I don't run to distractions.

I run to **stillness**.
To prayer.
To worship.
To journaling.
To breath.

Peace is no longer foreign—it's **home**.

Reflection

To the woman who feels uneasy in the calm—
You're not broken.
You're just learning how to exist without fear.

You've been in survival mode for so long,
but now, you're being invited to **thrive**.

So let peace in.

Let it settle into your bones.
Let it sing over your children.
Let it heal the places that never knew rest.

Because you were made for more than chaos.
You were made for joy, quiet, beauty, and breath.

Peace may have felt foreign once...
But now?
It's your native language.

A Letter to You, My Beautiful Sister

If you're reading these final pages, it means you didn't just survive—you showed up for yourself. You walked with me through heartbreak, healing, and the messy, beautiful road back to wholeness.

You may still feel like you're piecing yourself together.
You may still cry in silence or battle thoughts you don't share with anyone.
You may wonder if you'll ever fully feel safe, whole, or seen.

I've been there.

But I want to speak this into your soul: **There is nothing broken in you that God cannot restore.**

This book was not written from a place of perfection—it was written from the trenches. From the courtroom. From the tear-soaked pillow. From the strength I had to borrow from God when I had nothing left.

And I want you to know that healing is not a finish line—it's a sacred, daily journey. Some days you'll run. Some days you'll crawl. But every step is still a step forward.

You are not defined by what happened to you.
You are defined by the way you rise in spite of it.

This isn't the end of your story. It's the beginning of your becoming.

You were made for more.
More peace.
More joy.
More love.
More life.

So keep going, beautiful soul.
Hold your head high—not because everything is perfect, but because

you're still here.
That alone is victory.

With all my heart,
Milla Clervil
Author, Mother, Survivor, Daughter of the King

A Prayer to Seal Your Journey

God,
Continue the healing work You've started in her.
Restore what was lost.
Renew what was broken.
Revive what felt forgotten.
And remind her, every single day—
She is whole.
She is worthy.
She is deeply loved.

Amen.

Milla Clervil is a mother of six, a survivor of domestic violence, and a powerful voice for healing and restoration.

Through her books and her nonprofit work, she empowers women to rise from trauma, rediscover their worth, and embrace a life of peace, purpose, and love.

Love Again After Being a Survivor of Domestic Violence is her second book—a heartfelt journey of healing, faith, and transformation.

www.ingramcontent.com/pod-product-compliance
Lightning Source LLC
Chambersburg PA
CBHW020803130626
46554CB00006B/2303